KIDDING AROUND LONDON
A Family Guide to the City
Second Edition

Sarah Lovett

Illustrated by Michael Taylor

JOHN MUIR PUBLICATIONS • SANTA FE, NEW MEXICO

John Muir Publications, P.O. Box 613, Santa Fe, New Mexico 87504

Special Thanks:
Theo Pollon and Jade Sealey
Mary St. Clair's 6th grade class, Carlos Gilbert School, Santa Fe
Raphael, the coolest, Asana, Lauren, Joanne,
and Maloree's Junior School, London
Johanna, Tobias, Jemma, Sholla, Karen, Andy, Mali, Alexis,
Judy, Brian, David, Charlotte, Drake, Eda, Richard, Al, and
Donny, Natalie, Miriam and Marcia Joseph and Eleanor
Poland, Cathy Wren, Christopher Sykes, Kathleen Raine,
Ellen Feldman

Photo and text research, revision: John Liebson, P.J. Liebson

Library of Congress Cataloging-in-Publication Data
Lovett, Sarah, 1953-
Kidding around London: a family guide to the city / Sarah Lovett : illustrated by
Michael Taylor.—2nd ed.
    p.   cm.
Includes index.
ISBN 1-56261-224-7 : $9.95
1. London (England)—Guidebooks. 2. Family recreation—England—London—Guidebooks. 3.
Children—Travel—England—London—Guidebooks.
I. Taylor, Michael, 1953- . II. Title.
DA679.L85 1995
914.2104'859—dc20

94-44634
CIP

Production: Kathryn Lloyd-Strongin, Sarah Johansson
Editors: Dianna Delling, Elizabeth Wolf
Copy Editor: Jo Ann Baldinger
Designer and Typesetter: Linda Braun
Printer: Publishers Press, Salt Lake City, Utah

Cover Photo: Leo de Wys Inc./Steve Vidler

Distributed to the book trade by
Publishers Group West
Emeryville, California

Distributed to the education market by
Wright Group Publishing, Inc.
Bothell, Washington

CONTENTS

London is a marvelous place for families. You can walk underneath a river, get los
in a maze, tour dungeons and torture chambers, edit a film, and enjoy a laser
show. You can see some of the best theater in the world and watch a cricket game

GETTING TO KNOW LONDON

that lasts five days. You can eat Indian curry hot enough to sizzle your socks or
munch on English chips and catsup. You can explore great museums and wander
through palaces and castles. The only problem is finding the time to do everything

London Old and New

Capital of the United Kingdom, London is a city filled with history and tradition. When the pilgrims left England in 1620 and sailed to Plymouth Rock, London was already 1,577 years old. The city has a celebration or a memorial day for almost everything. There's a Druid ceremony to commemorate the spring equinox; a day in memory of Charles Dickens; and even one day each year when the Lord Mayor of London is presented with a boar's head on a silver platter, a tradition dating back to the 12th century.

In A.D. 43, Roman invaders founded a settlement they called Londinium on a sandy stretch of the Thames River. Throughout its long history, London has been home to kings and queens, artists, and politicians. It is the center of government for Great Britain and also a center for the arts and cultural affairs.

The Druids were the high priests of Celtic Britain

But London has also had its share of tragedy. Ninth century Viking warriors, in their quest for adventure and wealth, cruised up and down the river looting, burning, and generally causing trouble. The Great Plague killed 75,000 Londoners in 1665, and then on Sunday, September 1, 1666, a great fire destroyed 13,000 houses.

By 1800 London had a population of 1 million, making it the largest city in the Western world. At that time, slum children worked long hours in horrible sweatshops and factories, a practice that continued until child labor laws were enacted the end of the century. During World War II, more than 30,000 Londoners were killed in the Blitz, when German bombs destroyed much of the city.

London has also been the scene of cultural revolutions like the ones symbolized by the Beatles and the miniskirt in the 1960s, and rockers and punkers in the '70s and '80s.

London is filled with all kinds of people, including many whose families emigrated from former British colonies in Africa, Pakistan, India, and the West Indies. You'll hear many different languages spoken on the streets and see people of all colors and ethnic origins.

Londoners, in general, tend to be polite; like most of the English, they don't like to get "too personal." England has a definite class system, with the royal family and the aristocracy at the top and laborers and new immigrants at the bottom.

There's not much undeveloped land in London's crowded streets, but the city has many lush, green parks. You'll see a wide range of architectural styles. Older streets might look quaint and picturesque, with very narrow houses sharing common walls and lovely gardens. Some of the more recent buildings are just plain ugly, with starkly drab exteriors. ◆

How to Use This Book

The attractions in this book vary from historical landmarks to those involving sports and entertainment. Specific entry fees are generally not included because these change so quickly. Most fees are under £2, and many are less than 50 pence. Free entry is noted. Telephone numbers are included because it's always a good idea to ring first and double-check hours and fees. Chapters are divided by subject so you can pick and choose according to your interests.

England uses a 24-hour clock, so 1:00 p.m. would be called 13.00 hours in London. Very few times are included in the book because they are subject to change.

When possible, any pertinent information concerning special facilities for people with disabilities has been included. Again, telephone first. You'll find some helpful information on transportation in Chapter 3, Getting Around Town, and on using English money in Chapter 11, Shopping. Travel is one of the great adventures in life—so have a "smashing" time! ◆

During the Iron Age (roughly 1000 B.C.–A.D. 100), the tribal Celts roamed Europe on horseback. By the fifth century B.C., they controlled central Europe, Britain, and Ireland. The Druids' religious ceremonies are believed to have included animal sacrifices and magic.

Don't Forget Your Brolly In London it's a good idea to carry an umbrella at all times, although you may find the days are sunny and pleasantly warm, depending on the time of year. Rain or shine, it's always humid, and that's probably why London women are famous for their perfect complexions. ◆

London is famous for its "pea-soupers" (dense fog) and drizzling rain

IMPORTANT TELEPHONE NUMBERS

In the U.S.:
• British Tourist Authority, (800) 462-2748

In the U.K.:
• London Travel Service (travel, hotel & tour reservations), 01920/469755
• Visitorcall (information on events, theater, museums, transportation, shopping, etc.)
    a. 01839/123456 for menu of choices
    b. 01839/123424 for places of interest
      to children
• For emergency help, dial 999 from any phone (it's free) and ask for police, ambulance, or fire.

London was founded by the Romans nearly 2,000 years ago, and over the centuries has survived many hardships. But there

CHRONOLOGY

have been good times, too. Shakespeare, the Beatles, even royal weddings are part of the city's long and colorful history.

Saxon Chieftain

A Brief History of London

A.D.
43—When the Romans conquer Britain, they build a seaport on the Thames near the present-day London Bridge and name it Londinium.

61—Celtic tribesmen revolt against Nero's Roman rule.

61—The Romans build a wall around Londinium to protect it from raiders.

410—Roman troops withdraw from Britain to protect Gaul from invaders.

410–500—The Angles and the Saxons, two fierce, rival tribes, divide England into separate kingdoms.

700—Viking invasions and settlements.

825—The Saxons, who control London, gradually unite the rest of England into a single kingdom.

856—Alfred the Great restores London and makes it habitable.

King Henry VIII

Queen Elizabeth I

Mid-1000s—King Edward the Confessor, a Saxon, builds a palace and reconstructs a church about two miles southwest of London. These buildings are the beginning of the city of Westminster. The palace serves as the main residence of England's rulers until the 1520s; the church becomes Westminster Abbey.

1066—William the Conqueror, a Norman nobleman, takes control of England and crowns himself king in Westminster Abbey. He grants London self-government and builds himsel a castle, called the White Tower, just outside London, to remind Londoners of his power.

1100—London craft and trade guilds develop (bakers, goldsmiths, carpenters, and so on). Each guild has special uniforms and meeting halls.

1209—London Bridge, built of stone, replaces wooden bridges used by the Romans to cross the Thames.

1348—The bubonic plague, known as the "Black Death," devastates the city.

Late 1400s—London's population is about 50,000.

1509–1547—King Henry VIII rules England and owns six palaces in or near London.

1558–1603—Queen Elizabeth I helps London become an important world trade center.

1577—London's first theater, called simply The Theatre, opens outside the city walls. The crowds are rowdy, sometimes setting fire to the wooden seats.

1599—Shakespeare presents his plays at the Globe Theatre

Mid-1600s—London's population is 500,000. Most people live outside the city walls. Inside the walls, London is called the City.

1642—Civil war breaks out in England, pitting King Charles I against Parliament. London is pro-Parliament, led by Oliver Cromwell and other Puritans who oppose the luxury of the Church of England and the noble classes.

1649—The Puritans take control of the government and King Charles I loses his head.

1660—Parliament restores the monarchy and King Charles II is crowned.

1665—The Great Plague, a horrible epidemic of bubonic plague, ravages London and kills thousands of people.

1666, September 2—The Great Fire of London begins in a baker's shop on Pudding Lane and lasts five days. It destroys most of London, which is made of wood. A total of more than 80 churches and 13,000 houses burn to ashes, but no people are killed.

Late 1600s—London is rebuilt of stone and bricks. The famous architect, Sir Christopher Wren, designs the new St. Paul's Cathedral and many other structures.

1700s—London Stock Exchange is founded on Fleet Street.

1800—London's population reaches 1 million. It's the largest city in the Western world.

1800s—The age of the Industrial Revolution. London provides a great market for factory goods.

Mid-1800s—The City's merchants and bankers grow rich, and the West End of London is famous for a glittering social life. Meanwhile, the poor factory workers live in slums in the East End.

Last half of the 1800s—Reform laws are passed to help the working class.

1860s London Street Vendors

World War II

1840s to 1860s—Railroad stations are built around central London, including Victoria, King's Cross, and Paddington.

1863—London subway system opens.

1915—Germany bombs London during World War I.

September 1940–May 1941—During the London Blitz, Germany drops tons of bombs on the City and the East End. More than 30,000 Londoners are killed, and 80 percent of London's houses are damaged or destroyed.

1960—Skyscrapers are built in central London.

1962—The Beatles rise to stardom.

1970s—The Punk revolution rocks London.

1990—Margaret Thatcher's term as prime minister ends after 11 years.

1990—John Major elected prime minister.

1995—London's population is approximately 7 million.

The Beatles

You'll probably do lots of walking in London, but you also have three choices for public transportation: taxi, bus, or subway. Before you go anywhere, buy a copy of *AZ London Street Atlas*,

GETTING AROUND TOWN

the standard map book covering central London and the suburbs. You'll see Londoners carrying *AZ* under their arms, with the official underground (subway or tube) map on its back cover.

Public Transportation English **taxis** are different from American taxis. There's more leg room and they look very dignified. Of course, the driver sits on the *right* side. But just as in New York, if it's raining you'll never find a cab. If you're in a new part of town, ask where you should stand. People usually queue up and look for a taxi with its flag up or a for-hire sign.

The **buses** come in two layers: single-deckers and the picturesque double-deckers. If the bus is a front loader, you pay the driver exact fare as you climb aboard. If it's a bus with automatic doors at the tail-end, just jump on and a conductor will come around to collect fares and hand out tickets. Be alert—London bus routes are confusing, and the drivers are either very nice or very grumpy!

The **underground** train system is also called the **Tube**. It's a cheap and easy way to get about London. Many platforms have electric signs with train destinations listed. And there are easy maps of all the tube lines at every stop.

London is famous for its double-decker buses

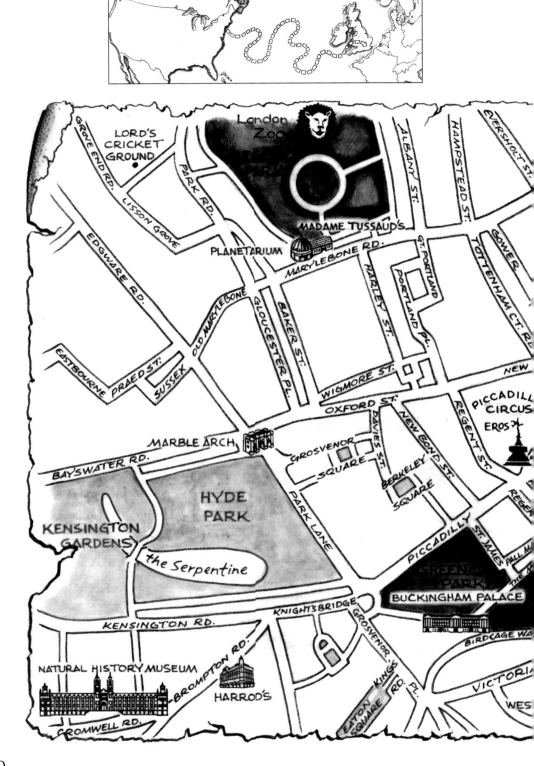

London has a population of 6,765,100 and occupies 693 square miles. It is located 3,458 miles from New York and 5,382 miles from Los Angeles.

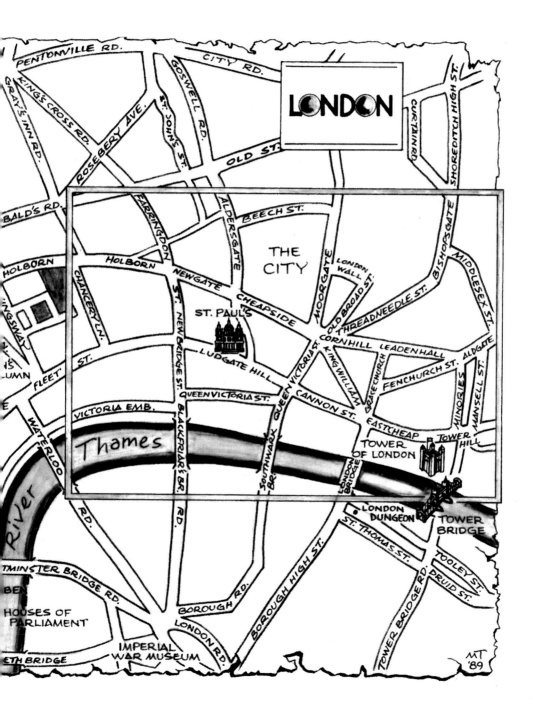

London Transport offers all sorts of deals. You can get special cards good for tubes, trains, and buses in Greater London and you can "swan" around all day, as the English say. There are other bargains if you just ask.

When you need information on London's buses or underground, call 0171-222 1234, 24 hours a day. That's the number of London Transport's **Travel Information Services**. There are offices at Victoria, Piccadilly Circus, King's Cross, Euston, Oxford Circus, St. James's Park, and Heathrow.

If you want to go out of town, **trains** are the way to travel. Train stations are right next to the tube stations. Oh, and don't forget to tell the kids that Paddington Bear got left behind in Paddington Train Station. For river transportation, call London Tourist Board, **Riverboat Information Services** at 0171-730 4812.

Whatever form of transportation you chose, remember: In Great Britain traffic moves on the opposite side of the street from the way it moves in the United States. Many roads are painted with reminders to "look left" or "look right." It will feel strange at first, so **be careful** when you're crossing streets. ◆

If you travel on London's Underground, you're likely to see "buskers"—musicians who play for spare change and literally sing for their supper. Buskers aren't the only people who "make" their meals in the tube. Like other big cities, London has many homeless people.

Buskers, or street musicians, brighten spirits even on London's most blustery days

London has long been the center of Great Britain's ruling powers. Since the Saxons (from Germany) and the Danes (from Denmark) ruled in the ninth century, England's

RULES AND ROYALTY

kings and queens have understood the need to command London. William the Conquerer began building the Tower of London in 1067 for that very reason.

British Politics Today the monarchy stands for protocol, ceremony, and the tradition of passing the crown down through the royal family. The "doings" of the royal family also provide Londoners with lots of entertaining gossip about how princes, princesses, and their friends spend their days.

Real political power belongs to Parliament instead of the royal family. Parliament is the national legislative governing body of Great Britain. It is composed of the House of Commons, whose members are democratically elected, and the House of Lords, who are usually members by birth. The prime minister and her or his cabinet rule the roost. There are two major political parties, the Conservative Party and the Labor Party.

London itself is divided into boroughs, or electoral districts, and each borough has its own distinct political personality. ◆

Buckingham Palace Buckingham Palace is a great place to begin exploring London. The present-day residence of the hereditary monarch, Buckingham Palace had its beginnings in the early 18th century, when the Duke of Buckingham built himself a brick house and called it Buckingham House. Later, George III tore down the library and built a ballroom, but it was George IV who, with architect John Nash, really went to town on the architecture. Victoria moved in later, as soon as she became queen, and the Royal Standard (flag) could be seen at the Marble Arch. (The Marble Arch was originally built by Nash for Buckingham Palace, but later it was moved to its present spot near Hyde Park.)

There are 40 acres of gardens at Buckingham Palace, filled with roses, herbs, a lake, and even pink flamingos. These days the palace is the home of Queen Elizabeth. You can tell she's in residence when the Royal Standard is flying. • Buckingham Palace: St. James's Park or Green Park tube stations; phone for hours; fee; 01-799 2331. ◆

You can identify the five regiments you'll see at Buckingham Palace by the plumes on their hats: white plume, the Grenadiers; scarlet plume, Coldstreams; buttons by threes and no plume, Scots; blue plume, Irish; and green and white plumes, Welsh

Be sure to catch the *Changing of the Guard*, the ceremony where the old Guard (soldiers who have been on duty) is replaced with the new. The soldiers' scarlet jackets were originally designed to hide the bloodstains of battle. Stand near the Queen Victoria Memorial or the center gates of the palace for the best view.

• Aug.–March, alternate days; April–July, every day. Guard leaves Wellington Barracks 11:00, arrives Buckingham Palace 11:30.

The **Royal Mews** is the Buckingham Palace stable. After their wedding in 1982, Prince Charles and Princess Diana returned to Buckingham Palace in a glass coach. That very coach is on display, along with the Gold State Coach (24 feet long, weighing 4 tons) and the Queen's Irish Coach. You can see the horses, too, unless they're out of the stable. • Oct.–March, Wednesdays; April–Oct., Tuesdays–Thursdays; closed 25–29 March, 1–5 Oct., 23 Dec.–5 Jan.; fee; 071-799 2331.

Big Ben, one of London's best-known landmarks, overlooks Parliament Square

While you're in *Parliament Square*, be sure to look up at *Big Ben*. The clock tower stands 316 feet tall. The bell was probably named after Sir Benjamin Hall, London's first commissioner of works, who was a very large man. The bell and clock were completed in 1858–59. When Parliament is "sitting" (in session), a light glows over Big Ben.

The Houses of Parliament

The borough of Westminster covers much of the West End and is the political core of London. It includes the Houses of Parliament, Whitehall, Westminster Cathedral, and Westminster Abbey.

The **Palace of Westminster** and the **Houses of Parliament** are one and the same, a dignified building in the Gothic style, characterized by pointed arches, steep roofs, and flying buttresses, right next to the Thames. Edward the Confessor (ruler 1042–1066) had the original palace built in honor of the French palaces he admired. Through the centuries, his buildings slowly disappeared because of fire damage and time. In 1835, architects Augustus Pugin and Charles Barry won a contest for a new palace design. Most of what you see today is their design. You won't be allowed to visit unless you know someone special to arrange a viewing; 071-219 3107.

William the Conqueror was crowned in **Westminster Abbey** on Christmas Day, 1066. Ever since, it's been the place where English monarchs are crowned. You can visit the abbey and make brass rubbings of historical figures. Choose your favorite brass from around the abbey. Then put the paper over the brass plaque and rub it with special crayons. The brass-rubbing center is open daily except Sunday. • Westminster Abbey: Westminster tube station; Monday–Saturday, Sunday for services only; closed weekdays to visitors during services; nave free, fee for Royal Chapels and Poets' Corner; limited handicapped access; 071-222 5152. ◆

Rub elbows with knights, queens, judges, and animals (all replicas of old church brass because too much rubbing wears away details on originals) at three London churches: St. James, All Hallows by the Tower, and St. Martin's in the Fields (where there are 90 replicas and new Celtic designs, and medieval music plays as you work). • London Brass Rubbing Centre: St. Martin's in the Fields, Trafalgar Square; Charing Cross tube station; daily except Good Friday, 24–26 Dec., 1 Jan.; fee; 0171-437 6023.

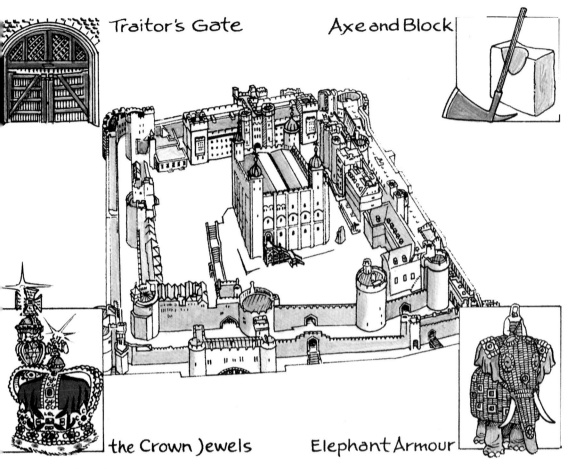

Traitor's Gate

Axe and Block

the Crown Jewels

Elephant Armour

The Tower of London is actually a series of several linked towers

The Tower   If you approach the Tower of London along the wall of the moat, you can see grass where there used to be water. For hundreds of years the moat was full of filthy water. It was originally supposed to fill with fresh water at high tide and to be cleaned as the tide went out. But the moat was built lower than the Thames, and it never emptied out. That wouldn't have been so bad except it was loaded with trash, animal carcasses, and sewage from the town of London. So the moat was drained in 1843, and these days it's a garden.

Located on almost 18 acres of land, the Tower of London is actually many towers linked by walls. It began as a fortress when William the Conqueror wanted to impress the people of London with his power. In later years the tower was used as the Royal Mint, an arsenal, and even a zoo where King Henry VIII kept his exotic animals.

The **White Tower**, near the center, is the oldest tower of the fortress, dating back to 1078. It took 20 years to build, and its walls are 100 feet high. The White Tower houses a collection of lances, crossbows, pistols, and other weapons on the first floor.

The Tower of London is most famous as a prison for political inmates. Those who threatened the king often spent their last days imprisoned inside the fortress.

Don't miss Traitors' Gate, where unfortunate prisoners were brought secretly by boat in the dead of night. You can also see a wooden execution block and the ax used for beheadings.

One look at the gray stones of the **Bloody Tower** and you can almost hear the moans and groans of ghostly prisoners. The Bloody Tower got its name from the story of the murder of two little princes. When Edward IV died in 1483, his two sons, 12-year-old Prince Edward and his younger brother, Richard, Duke of York, were housed in the tower to await young Edward's coronation. But their uncle, Richard III, became king instead, and the little princes, left alone in the tower, were forgotten. Many people believe that Richard III had them murdered so he could become king. In 1674 the bones of two children were discovered buried close to the tower.

You can spend all day at the Tower of London and you still won't see it all. At the Royal Armouries, look for the world's biggest set of armor (made for an Indian elephant), along with armor for a giant and a dwarf. And then there's the Duke of Wellington's barracks, where you'll now find the Crown Jewels, including the largest cut diamond in the world. (The Queen is rumored to refer to the Crown Jewels as "Granny's Chips.")

Have someone take a photo of you standing next to a Beefeater. Beefeaters are special guards for the tower and were originally appointed by King Edward VI. The Beefeaters also offer scheduled tours of the tower. • Tower: Tower Hill tube station; Nov.–Feb., Monday–Saturday; March–Oct., daily; closed Good Friday, 24–25 Dec., 1 Jan; fee; limited handicapped access; 071-709 0765. Just outside the Tower, within 30 feet of the souvenir shop, are docks where you can board a boat to sail downriver to Greenwich or the Thames Flood Barriers. (More about that in Chapter 9, Rivers and Bridges.) ◆

Beefeaters stand guard outside the Tower of London

Legend has it that without its resident ravens, the Tower would fall—and so would the kingdom

The tower has always been home to **ravens**. These days, the ravens are brought especially from Scotland, Wales, and the west of England. Their wings are clipped so they can't fly. When they die they're buried in a special raven cemetery in the empty moat.

The Ceremony of the Keys

Don't miss the Ceremony of the Keys, which symbolizes nine centuries of the Tower of London's league with British monarchy and history. Each night at 9:40 (21.40 hours), the Chief Yeoman Warder of the Tower—sporting a red cloak and Tudor bonnet—carries the keys of the fortress toward Byward Tower.

"An escort for the Keys," he calls, and four soldiers of the Brigade of Guards join his march. The West Gates, the Middle Tower, and Byward Tower are locked. As the Chief Warder approaches the Bloody Tower, a sentry calls out a challenge.

"Halt, who goes there?"

"The Keys."

"Whose Keys?"

"Queen Elizabeth's Keys," the Chief Yeoman Warder of the Tower cries. "God preserve Queen Elizabeth."

One of the world's oldest military ceremonies ends with *Amens* all round. • In advance, for free passes write to the Yeoman Clerk, Queen's House, HM Tower of London, London EC3N 4AB, England. ◆

Yeomen partake in one of the world's oldest military ceremonies

Hampton Court In 1515 Thomas Wolsey, a very ambitious man, began building a Tudor-style palace with 1,000 rooms and 280 silk beds. Tudor is a style of architecture that was developed during the reign of the Tudor family (1485–1603). Tall chimneys, gables, arches, mullioned windows, and paneled walls distinguish Tudor architecture from that of the Middle Ages. Wolsey called the house Hampton Court and presented it to King Henry VIII (ruler 1509–1547) as a gift.

The high green hedges of Hampton Court Maze, planted and trimmed in a geometrical pattern, make it easy to get lost. Give yourself plenty of time to find the center because it can take as long as 20 minutes. (And then you have to get out!) • Daily; last admission one hour before closing. Separate fee for palace and maze. Limited handicapped access.

Henry moved into the palace part-time, along with the 1,000 people of his royal household. Henry remodeled and enlarged the palace so he'd have more room.

In 1689 architect Christopher Wren made major changes to Hampton Court in the Baroque style, which is characterized by the heavy use of swirls and ornamentation, for King William III and Queen Mary. William and Mary loved the gardens, and together with Wren, planned the **"Wilderness" garden**, where you'll find the famous maze. All the gardens at Hampton Court are spectacular. Trees are trimmed to resemble giant toadstools, roses bloom in impossible colors, and in the 1800s the famous grapevine produced more than 2,000 pounds of grapes per year.

You can wander around inside the palace and view the state rooms, the dining room, and the giant kitchen where vast meals were prepared. You'll see paintings by such artists as Jan Breughel and Jacopo Tintoretto. In the Clock Court, near the center of the palace, look for the astronomical clock that was made especially for King Henry. Notice the Earth is the center of the "solar system." There's also a restaurant, the

Hampton Court Maze is a real-life labyrinth of tall green hedges

Haunted Gallery (where the ghost of Henry's fifth wife, Catherine Howard, is said to wander), and the **Cartoon Gallery** (the word "cartoon" originally meant a finished sketch for a painting) with tapestry cartoons by Raphael. • Hampton Court: by train from Waterloo Station to Hampton Court Station or by boat from Westminster, Charing Cross, or Tower Bridge Piers; open daily, except Good Friday, 24–25 Dec., and 1 Jan.; fee for state apartments and maze; 0181-977 8441. ◆

Windsor Castle   If you've ever dreamed of living in an enchanted fairy-tale castle with turrets and towers, then you'll love Windsor Castle. William the Conqueror's original wooden castle was a very modest place. But through the years it's been enlarged and rebuilt in stone, until today it seems to fill the sky with golden magic. As you approach the main gate, stop a moment and imagine the days of knights and chivalry.

During the last 900 years, almost every English ruler has lived in Windsor Castle. Even today the royal family stays in residence part of the year, on weekends or holidays. Outside, on the grounds, is St. George's Chapel, where King Henry VIII is buried. Inside the castle you can view paintings and drawings and a great collection of armor. The castle was damaged by fire in November 1992; some restoration may still be in progress, but all areas have been reopened. Visiting Windsor Castle is a good excuse to take a train. You can leave London from Paddington Station. The trip takes about 35 minutes. • Windsor Castle: fee; 01753-868 286. ◆

Don't miss the **Queen's Dollhouse** in Windsor Castle. It was given to Queen Mary in 1923, and it's a perfect palace within a palace. The electric lights really work, and you can lock the doors with keys. There are even "lifts" to take tiny visitors to other floors, and a library with more than 200 tiny books especially written for "small" readers.

The suits worn by the Cockney royalty are covered with pearl buttons

The Legend of King Arthur

According to the legend of King Arthur and the Knights of the Round Table, Arthur was the illegitimate son of King Pendragon. When the king died, Arthur alone could pull the sword, Excalibur, from the stone. Then Merlin, the court magician, told Arthur about his royal parentage. King Arthur and his knights became famous for courage and chivalry. ◆

The Pearly King and Queen

London has more than one kind of royalty. "Cockney" is a popular term for working-class people from the East End of London. But true Cockneys must be born within the sound of London's Bow Church bells. Their own royalty, called Pearly Kings and Queens, are famous for wearing special suits and dresses covered with thousands of tiny pearl buttons. Although Pearly Kings and Queens have no official political power, they are very important to the Cockneys. ◆

The legend of King Arthur and the Knights of the Round Table originated in sixth century Britain

Although much of London was destroyed
by German bombs in World War II, almost all
the ruins have disappeared under new

WAR AND REVOLUTION

buildings and developments. Even so, many
older Londoners are veterans of the war and
lost friends and family in the carnage.

Cabinet War Rooms The Cabinet War Rooms lie 7 feet under the earth. Here you'll find the most important part of the underground emergency accommodation created to protect Winston Churchill, his war cabinet, and the chiefs of staff of Britain's armed forces during the brutal air attacks. The 19 rooms on view include the Cabinet Room, where many of the crucial decisions of World War II were made; the Transatlantic Telephone Room, where Churchill spoke directly to President Roosevelt in the White House; the Map Room, used to keep track of all war fronts; and the Prime Minister's Room, where Churchill made his famous wartime broadcasts. The Cabinet War Rooms are maintained to give you a real sense of what it was like to be in the nerve center of the war effort. • Cabinet War Rooms: Clive Steps, King Charles Street; Westminster tube station; daily except Good Friday, May Day, 24–26 Dec., 1 Jan.; fee; 0171-930 6961. ◆

Around the corner from the Cabinet War Rooms you can follow Horse Guards Road to the **Horse Guards**. The Guard mounts at 11:00 (10:00 Sundays) daily in ceremonial splendor at Horse Guards Parade (Whitehall) in summer and the courtyard in winter.

People Power Trafalgar Square has been a popular setting for political rallies since the 1820s. Fifty thousand people can gather there at once to let their voices and opinions be heard. It was designed by John Nash (the same person who worked on Buckingham Palace) to celebrate the British naval victory over France and Spain at Trafalgar in 1805. There's a great Christmas tree there during the holidays, and you can always hear Big Ben chime clearly. It's also a famous place for pigeons to hang out. • Trafalgar Square: Charing Cross tube station. ◆

Nelson's Column stands tall in Trafalgar Square

Royal Hospital Soldiers are a living reminder of formal power and war. Enter the black and gold gates of the Royal Hospital, Chelsea, and you'll see pensioners (retired soldiers) in red or blue uniforms with two rows of buttons and tall, noble hats on their heads. Some of them are very talkative and don't mind questions. Visit the fabulous Great Hall where they take tea. There's a colorful mural of Charles II on one wall and the many tables are formally set with small green lamps.

Directly across from the Great Hall you'll find the **Chapel**, with special pillows set out on the benches. Each pillow has the insignia of a different regiment. The Royal Engineers have a bright red design with green laurel leaves. In the area outside the Chapel look for the flags taken from different battles displayed on the walls. Outdoors in the garden green is a statue of Charles II who laid the foundation stone of the hospital in 1682. Designed by Sir Christopher Wren, the Royal Hospital also houses a museum with a collection of almost 2,000 medals. • Royal Hospital: Royal Hospital Road. Sloane Square tube station; daily; closed national holidays and Sundays Oct.–March; disabled access; 0171-730 0161. ◆

Nearly 400 pensioners now live at the Royal Hospital

The City Within the City   Inside London is one-square-mile area called the **City of London**, a strategic center of world financial affairs. At least a third of this area was destroyed by bombs in World War II, but you won't see any evidence because it's all been rebuilt. Barbican Centre, an arts complex completed in 1982, is one of the more recent changes. The area of Barbican was completely flattened during the Blitz, except for St. Giles Church of Cripplegate. The church still stands in the middle of Barbican Centre, which is the home of the Royal Shakespeare Company (see Chapter 10, That's Entertainment). • Barbican Centre: Barbican tube station. ◆

WAR MUSEUMS AND EXHIBITS

The Imperial War Museum
chronicles the history of war in the 20th century. The museum has been extensively remodeled, and new exhibits include "The Blitz Experience."
• Imperial War Museum: Lambeth Rd. Lambeth North or Elephant and Castle tube stations; daily except 24–26 Dec., 1 Jan.; fee; 0171-416 5000.

The Guards Museum
is an exceptional place where the entire family will enjoy learning about the five Foot Guards Regiments.
• Guards Museum: Wellington Barracks, Birdcage Walk. St. James's Park tube station; daily except Friday and national holidays; fee; 0171-930 4466, ext. 3430.

The Royal Air Force Museum
has more than 65 aircraft and other equipment on exhibit, and includes the Battle of Britain Museum.
• Royal Air Force Museum: Grahame Park Way, Herndon; Conlindale tube station; daily except 25–26 Dec., 1 Jan.; fee; 0181-205 2266.

The HMS Belfast
was one of the largest cruisers in the Royal Navy and saw action during the D-Day landings. It is displayed along with an Imperial War Museum exhibit about the Royal Navy from 1914 to the present.
• HMS Belfast: Morgan's Lane, Tooley Street. Monument, Tower or London Bridge tube stations; daily except 24–26 Dec., 1 Jan.; fee; 0171-407 6434. ◆

Throughout its history, London has been
the backdrop for some of life's darker
aspects: torture, grave robbing, plague,

ODD AND CREEPY THINGS

and witchcraft. Modern London offers
you the chance to learn about some of
the creepier moments of history.

Historical House of Wax

Madame Tussaud (1761–1850) was a very unusual woman. She worked at the court of Louis XVI making wax figures, an art she learned from her uncle. She was sent to prison during the French Revolution, and there she made death masks modeled from the heads of actual guillotine victims, including King Louis XVI and Marie Antoinette. In 1802 she took her children and her wax models to England.

The first thing you'll probably see at **Madame Tussaud's Wax Museum** is a very long line. The summer season is the worst for crowds, but even in winter tourists flock to this famous wax museum. The entry chamber is filled with historical tableaus like the famous little princes in their royal prison (see Chapter 3, Rules and Royalty). Most of the faces at Madame Tussaud's are fairly lifelike, but the hands are even better.

Things get more interesting in the other chambers, where you often can't tell the crowds of tourists from the wax figures. Joan Collins (who doesn't look very real) shares the stage with the Beatles, Michael Jackson, Benjamin Franklin, and John F. Kennedy. Then comes the **Chamber of Horrors**. As you descend the stone staircase, a loud, gloomy bell tolls in your ear.

*Henry VIII and his six wives are among the lifelike
wax figures displayed at Madame Tussaud's*

Courtesy of the British Tourist Authority

The chamber smells of gunpowder, and you're overwhelmed by the sounds of gunshots and the zap of the electric chair. The guillotine is stained with blood. Madame Tussaud herself modeled Jean Paul Marat, the French revolutionary, after he was murdered in his bath.

Other sights at the museum include a foggy, gaslit London street where Jack the Ripper hangs out. Something new at Tussaud's: the dark "Spirit of London" ride, where you can time-travel via taxi into London's past. • Madame Tussaud's: Marylebone Rd.; Baker St. tube station; daily; fee 0171-935 6861. ◆

Right next door to Madame Tussaud's are the **London Planetarium** and the **Laserium**, with its newest attraction, the "Space Trail." By day, gaze at 9,000 stars, moons, and planets created with a Zeiss projector that has 20,000 separate parts. In the early evening the same equipment is used along with rock and pop music for a laser show. If you're in the mood to spend the day, you can buy combination tickets for Madame Tussaud's, the Planetarium, and Laserium. • Planetarium and Laserium: daily; fee (over age 5 only); 0171-486 1121; ring in advance if you need assistance for disabled persons; ring Laserline for show information, 0171-486 2242.

A gruesome guillotine welcomes you to the Chamber of Horrors

Walk down Marylebone Road from Madame Tussaud's, turn the corner, and you're on Baker Street, home of the great Victorian fictional detective Sherlock Holmes, created by Sir Arthur Conan Doyle. Holmes' address, 221B Baker Street, has really existed since the street was renumbered in 1930. But you will have to sleuth out the reminders of the gas lamps and hansom cabs that existed in his day.
• 071-935 8866.

Down and Dirty Another haven for aficionados of the appalling is the **London Dungeon**. Located in the vaults beneath London Bridge Station, here you can return to the days of torture, witchcraft, and disease. Life-size exhibits, complete with smells, sights, and sounds, depict almost every disgusting aspect of British medieval history. There's also a newly opened exhibit of Pudding Lane, where the Great Fire of London started on September 1, 1666. The dungeon is not for unaccompanied kids, children under 10, or anyone with a queasy stomach. • London Dungeon: 28/34 Tooley Street; daily except 24–26 Dec.; fee; limited handicapped access, telephone in advance for assistance; not recommended for young children; 171-403 0606. ◆

The underground London Dungeon presents an eerie overview of British medieval history

Of Grave Interest

A good old-fashioned cemetery is a perfect place for a scare, and **Highgate Cemetery**, now a nature reserve, is one of the best. Be sure to enter the famous Egyptian Gates and wander up Egyptian Avenue, where it looks like a mummy will appear any minute. When you reach the Catacombs you might be able to peer through a crack in the mossy stones into the underground tombs. And look on top of the Circle of Lebanon for the amazing cypress tree that spreads its branches over the circular-patterned tombs.

Enter Highgate Cemetery through the famous Egyptian Gates

The western portion of Highgate Cemetery was opened by the London Cemetery Company in 1839 because London's church graveyards were full. In 1854 the Eastern Cemetery was opened, and the fashionable society of Victorian London used to stroll past the numerous tombs, vaults, and monuments on Sunday afternoons. It was the place to see and be seen.

• Highgate Cemetery: East side open daily; fee; west side by guided tour only; weekdays, some weekends; fee; closed 25 Dec. and for funerals; 0181-340 1834. Directions: Take the Northern Line of the London underground to Archway. From there you can walk up Highgate Hill, cros through Waterlow Park and stop for tea, and continue your walk (five to ten minutes) to the cemetery. Hampstead Heath is also in the same neighborhood (Chapter 7, Parks and Gardens). ◆

There are two sides to the cemetery: the Western Cemetery, where writer Charles Dickens's wife, Catherine, and eight-month-old daughter, Dora, are buried, and the Eastern Cemetery, where you'll find Karl Marx's tomb and monument.

Nursery Rhyme That's Not-so-Nice

Ring a-ring a-Rosies
A pocketful of posies,
'Tishoo,' 'tishoo,'
We all fall down!

This nursery rhyme is anything but merry. It dates back to the Great Plague that raged through London in 1665. A pink "rosie" skin rash signaled the dreaded plague. Posies were supposed to protect you, sneezing ('tishoo') meant sure death, and falling down was how you died. ◆

Horniman Museum

Horniman Museum has a striking art nouveau facade and exhibits of ethnography and natural history. Note the Cult of the Dead section, mummies, and an ancient Egyptian tomb. There's also an aquarium and a colony of honey bees. Horniman: 100 London Rd., by train to Forest Hill station and taxi to museum. Monday–Saturday; free; 0181-699 1872. ◆

The Un-Circus

Piccadilly Circus, Soho, is *not* a circus! It's where Piccadilly Street and Regent Street intersect. In the old days, they converged in a circular pattern. Today a statue of Eros, the god of love, presides over this busy intersection in the West End.

The Trocadero, at Shaftesbury Avenue and Coventry Street, offers modern mall conveniences: shopping, eating, and entertainment. That's where you'll find **The Guinness World of Records**, two floors of life-size exhibits featuring the world's fattest, tallest, shortest, and some of the weirdest. Plastic models show off Arnold Schwarzenegger's "best body" and nature's biggest vegetables. One of GWR's highlights is a scale with the fattest man on one side. Kids get together and climb on the other side to see how many of them it takes to balance

Courtesy of the British Tourist Authority

Piccadilly is a busy London intersection, not an actual circus

Your favorite British rock stars come to life at Rock Circus

the weight. • Guinness World of Records: Piccadilly Circus tube station; daily except 25 Dec.; fee; 0171-439 7331. ◆

Call the Ghost Busters!

London has more than its share of haunted houses. Hampton Court has a haunted gallery, where two wives of Henry VIII have been seen wandering around: Jane Seymour, who died in childbirth, carries a candle and moans sadly, while Catherine Howard, who eventually had her head chopped off, is said to rush around trying to find King Henry and plead her case. Elephant and Castle tube station is known for strange clankings and footsteps. The British Museum, renowned for mummies dating back to 4500 B.C., also boasts a ghost dressed as an Egyptian princess.

Rock Circus rocks with replicas of rock stars, rock music, and lasers. It's an offshoot of Madame Tussaud's, in the London Pavilion at Piccadilly Circus. • Rock Circus: daily except 25 Dec.; fee; 0171-734 8025.)

Another ghost—a Victorian actor who was murdered—haunts Covent Garden tube station and the Adelphi Theatre, where he worked. ◆

OTHER ODD NOTABLES

The Monument
(on Monument St.) qualifies as the world's tallest isolated stone tower. It also marks the place where the great London fire started. Designed by Sir Christopher Wren, the tower is 202 feet high and is located 202 feet from the site of the fire's origin.
• The Monument: Monument tube station.

Chiselhurst Caves
is the place to explore an old chalk mine (possibly Roman) via guided, lamplit tours.
• Old Hill, Chiselhurst: by train to Chiselhurst; Oct.–Easter, weekends; Easter–Sept., daily; fee; 0181-467 3264.

Tower Hill Pageant
offers a dark ride into London's history, complete with smells and sound effects.
• Tower Hill Terrace: Tower Hill tube station; daily except Christmas Day; fee; 0171-709 0081.

The Whispering Gallery
in St. Paul's Cathedral is not a place for telling secrets! It's an acoustic wonder where quiet sounds travel 107 feet.
• Ludgate Hill: St. Paul's tube station; Monday–Saturday, closed occasionally; fee; 0171-248 2705.

Parks are inexpensive, democratic, and often surprising places to spend a lazy afternoon or even an entire day. Take time out to fly a

PARKS AND GARDENS

kite, talk to the animals at the London Zoo, or simply relax with a blanket and a good book—one of Shakespeare's plays, perhaps?

Park Yourself   If you stepped into a time machine and zipped back three centuries, you'd find people strolling around **Hyde Park** almost like they do today. Hyde Park encompasses more than 300 acres of grass, trees, gardens, and even a lake. It has been the scene of horse races, duels, and royal hunts.

But **Speaker's Corner**, near Marble Arch, has only been around since 1872, when the government earmarked this unassuming spot for free speech and public debate. You'll find men and women of all persuasions and philosophies standing on soapboxes and preaching eloquently to the interested crowds. The subject could be anything, but religion is especially popular, and spectators join the debate whenever they fe bold enough. • Hyde Park: Hyde Park Corner tube station.

An easy stroll through Hyde Park—past equestrians, soccer games, people loung ing in folding chairs, and babies in strollers takes you to **The Serpentine**, a small lake where you can rent a rowboat or a paddlebo take a dip (*brrrrr*), or feed the waterfowl.

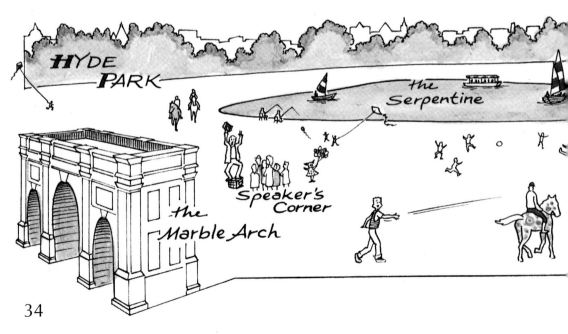

HYDE PARK

the Serpentine

Speaker's Corner

the Marble Arch

It's difficult to tell where Hyde Park ends and **Kensington Gardens** begins. It doesn't really matter because they're both green and lovely, and together they cover 600 acres. But the tail end of The Serpentine lake becomes **The Long Water** (a narrow curve of water) and then you're in the gardens.

Continue west toward the Children's Playground and the Elfin Oak, where colorful finger-sized elves romp and play in the old tree trunk. • Hyde Park: Hyde Park Corner and Lancaster Gate tube stops.

Regent's Park is one of the biggest in central London. There are rose gardens, boats to hire, and plenty of room for sports like cricket, football, and lacrosse. During the summer you may happen upon music or other entertainment in the open-air theater.

Regent's Park is home to the **London Zoo**, founded in 1826, and its 8,000 creatures. Favorite exhibits include the giant panda, lions, tigers, and the Reptile House filled with alligators and snakes. The miracle of technology and reversed lighting has created **Moonlight World**, where spiny

anteaters, bats, and kiwis do their stuff in the "dark of night" while you watch in daylight! Of special interest are feeding time, camel and llama rides, and daily animal shows. Don't miss the Zoo Waterbus on the Grand Union Canal, one of the best ways to see exotic zoo creatures from April to September. • London Zoo: Camden Town tube stop, then watch for specially marked buses to the zoo; daily except 25 Dec.; fee; 0171-722 3333. ◆

At Kensington Gardens, try to spot the elves at the Elfin Oak

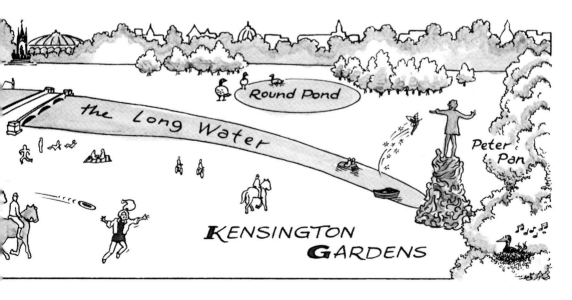

the Long Water

Round Pond

Peter Pan

KENSINGTON GARDENS

Something on your mind? Stop by the Speaker's Corner and get it off your chest!

You'll find the famous statue of **Peter Pan** by Sir G. Frampton at the edge of The Long Water in Hyde Park, where Peter first landed his boat in Sir James Barrie's 1904 play. Take some time to examine the delightful details in the base of the sculpture.

It's easy to make friends with the hungry geese at Hyde Park

Courtesy of the British Tourist Authority

ew Gardens You can take a guided tour or wander on your own through almost 300 acres of exotic plants, trees, and flowers at Kew Gardens. These Royal Botanical Gardens grew from a humble beginning of seven acres before Princess Augusta decided to enlarge things in the mid-1700s. Plant houses include the refrigerated Alpine House, the Australian House, and the Tropical Waterlily House, where you'll be dwarfed by giant lily pads. Leave yourself lots of time to explore the gardens outside, where you'll find azaleas, Japanese cherries, a bamboo garden, and some very rare plant species. The Princess of Wales Conservatory, with ten climatic zones, is new and wonderful.

The Royal Residence, **Kew Palace**, near the main gates (open April to Sept., daily), was built by Samuel Fortrey in the early 1600s. (It's also known as the Dutch House because Fortrey's ancestors came from Holland.) Behind Kew Palace you'll find a small kitchen garden. Queen Charlotte, who raised her children in the royal residences, designed a quaint picnic cottage called (not surprisingly) the **Queen's Cottage** (1772). Upstairs you'll find tea for two set out invitingly, but before you sit down, remember, it's a museum. You can find your own refreshments at the pavilion.

• Kew Gardens: Kew Gardens tube station; daily; fee; arrive at least two hours before closing; 0181-940 1171. ◆

At Kew Gardens, visit the Great Pagoda for a taste of China

Hampstead Heath   Hampstead Heath is another large park (800 acres). It wasn't always a park—maids from wealthy homes in the neighborhood used to lay the laundry out to dry here. Find a high spot like Parliament Hill (319 feet above sea level) for a super view of London. It's also a terrific place to fly kites or ride a toboggan.

The heath is great for birdwatching, so bring your binoculars. And don't forget a swimming suit; even in winter, very brave folks go out to crack the ice on the ponds before they take a dip. If you happen to have a fishing rod handy, you can cast out in the pond nearest Parliament Hill.

• Hampstead Heath is close to Highgate Cemetery (see Chapter 6, Odd and Creepy Things). Take the tube to the Hampstead station and then catch a bus. Ask for directions at the tube station. ◆

The Greenwich Meridian, an imaginary line spanning the globe from the North Pole to the South Pole, is the theoretical center of the world's standard time zone system

Greenwich Park The town of Greenwich is filled with picturesque buildings, winding streets, and pretty gardens. It sits right on the edge of the Thames, and its shops, restaurants, and museums surround Greenwich Park.

From the National Maritime Museum (Chapter 8, Museums), walk through the park to the top of the hill and the Old Royal Observatory. Make sure you arrive at the Old Royal Observatory by 13.00 hours so you can set your watch by the falling timeball. Then stand astride the brass Meridian Zero. Greenwich was selected in 1884 as the prime, or zero, meridian. All other north/south longitudinal lines are measured from this point. • Greenwich: by train from Charing Cross station to Maze Hill; by boat from Westminster, Charing Cross, or Tower Bridge Piers. ◆

Battersea Park Battersea Park, across the Thames from Chelsea, is 200 acres of wide-open fun. It's a great place to find special events like fairs, open-air concerts, and dancing. There's a children's zoo and a snack stand near the boating lake. • Battersea Park: Sloan Square tube station, then take the bus to the first stop south of the river. Battersea Arts Centre is mostly accessible for disabled; telephone in advance; 0171-223 8413. ◆

The gardens at *Hampton Court* (Chapter 4, Rules and Royalty) are sensational: roses, rare plants, and formal courtyards with charming fountains. Of course, take time to explore Hampton Court Maze.

The world is full of fabulous creations, and London's museums hold more than their fair share—from mummies and medieval treasures to fabulous gemstones and high-tech movie-making

MUSEUMS

equipment. Look and learn about history, or actually try your hand at a science experiment. If you're the least bit curious, you'll enjoy visiting one of the city's museums.

Hands-on Science Fun

Not too far from Hyde Park you could spend days viewing and participating in some of the great discoveries of humankind. **The Science Museum** offers a mind-boggling array of exhibits. Choose from oil, steam, wind, and turbine engines (Galleries Two and Three), exploration in space and the Apollo 10 capsule (Gallery Six), or Puffing Billy, the oldest locomotive in the world.

Upstairs, the **Launch Pad** offers opportunities to interact with displays like the grain loader, where you can climb aboard and send buckets of wheat along the loading belt for grinding and processing. You can hold up what looks like a ray gun and color your own video image on a TV screen. The darkroom

When you visit the Launch Pad, have a shocking experience!

guarantees sparks with glowing globes, electric rays, and heat sensors. • Science Museum: daily, closed 24–26 Dec., 1 Jan.; fee; 0171-938 8000. Some disabled access, telephone in advance. ◆

Natural Wonders

You don even have to come up for air to find the **Natural History Museum**. It's an ea walk from the Science Museum's below-ground level through the Centre Hall with all the locomotives.

Popular exhibi include "Discovering Mammals," with a life-size model of a blue whale The "Human Biology" exhibit uses interactiv computer technolog to show how your body works. If you're visiting during British

The Natural History Museum building also houses the Geological Museum

school holidays (August and two weeks of Easter), head for the Discovery Center. Past exhibits included a chick hatchery, a giant model of a mole tunnel with a humongous worm, and a display of hundreds of live butterflies. The Ecology exhibit complete with rain forest is new; so are the life-size moving dinosaurs and "Creepies Crawlies."

The **Geological Museum** is housed in the East Wing of the Natural History Museum. The incredible story of the Earth is on view here with rare rock specimens, relief models, photographs, and maps. For those who love shiny and expensive things, there's the world-famous gemstone collection—diamonds, emeralds, sapphires, and rubies. The Earthquake Machine is new and shocking!

Diplodocus carnegii stands proudly, all 26 meters of him, in the spectacular central hall of the Natural History Museum. He's a plaster cast of the original dinosaur skeleton dating back 150 million years. Before you leave the main hall, look for the stone monkeys climbing the corners of the room.

• Natural History Museum Complex: daily; fee, except near the end of the day; limited handicapped access, telephone in advance; 171-938-9123. ◆

The Natural History Museum's dinosaur skeleton was originally discovered in Wyoming!

Next door, the **Victoria and Albert Museum** features displays of medieval art, musical instruments, and treasures from the Far East. There are completely furnished rooms from different periods of history, like an 18th-century music room, a Gothic room, and a room from a 17th-century inn. The Raphael gallery and the glass gallery (showing the 4,000-year history of glass) are two new additions. • Victoria and Albert: daily except Good Friday, May Day, 24–26 Dec., 1 Jan.; fee; 0171-938 5800.

Lights, Camera, Action!

At **MOMI**, the **Museum of the Moving Image**, there are more than 50 exhibits about film in which you can participate to your heart's content. Why not try your hand at editing? You can anchor the TV evening news or give an interview to Barry Norman, London's famous weekly TV and film critic. A videotape of Norman asks you questions, you answer, and technicians put the two of you together on the spot. Presto, instant interview.

MOMI is staffed with actors, actresses, and technicians ready to answer questions. For a flash from the past you can visit a real "picture house" from the 1930s. An usher escorts you to your seat spouting local cockney chat. If you're an animation freak, you can study the 18th- and 19th-century animation machines and make your own cartoons. Just draw your character on a strip of paper, put paper inside the Zoetrope animation machine, spin it, and watch the action. Plan to spend all day at MOMI, but take a lunch; there are no food facilities. • MOMI: South Bank; Waterloo tube station; daily except 24–26 Dec.; fee; disabled access, telephone in advance; 01-401 2636. ◆

If you've always wanted to fly, at MOMI you can lie on a slanted board and whizz over the rooftops of London. The secret is the same blue background that is used in Superman movies.

The Elgin marbles, from the Acropolis in
Athens, Greece, date to the fourth century B.C.

Mum's the Word The **British Museum** is full of the wonders of many civilizations. The Egyptian mummies are not to be missed. Neither are the Rosetta Stone, covered with ancient hieroglyphics, or the Elgin marbles, fourth century sculptures from the Acropolis in Athens. The marbles are controversial because Thomas Bruce, seventh earl of Elgin, spent time in Greece and collected many works of art that were in danger of being destroyed. In 1816 he sold the Elgin marbles to the British government for half of what they cost him. How many people believe they should be returned to Greece because they're part of Greek history and culture.

Another incredible place to see is the museum's Reading Room. Scholars come from all over the world to use this library. • British Museum: Great Russell St. Holborn or Tottenham Court Rd. tube stations; daily except

Good Friday, May Day, 23-26 Dec., Jan. 1; free, fee for guided tour; handicapped access, telephone in advance; 0171-636 1555 or 580 1788 for recorded info. ◆

Ships Ahoy For ships, the ocean, and naval history, nothing beats the **National Maritime Museum** in Greenwich Park (Chapter 7, Parks and Gardens). The museum is impressive on the outside and fascinating on the inside. You enter the grounds through the beautiful black and gold Royal Gates. Museum buildings include the glorious Queen's House, designed by the great English architect, Inigo Jones. Ship models, maritime artifacts and memorabilia, and actual boats are displayed inside. You can learn about Lord Nelson (1758–1805), who defeated the French and Spanish fleets at Trafalgar

Outside the National Maritime Museum is a dolphin sundial on which time is told to the minute by shadowy dolphin tails

but was mortally wounded; Sir Francis Drake (1540–1596), the first Englishman to circumnavigate the world; and Captain James Cook (1728–1779), who explored Australia and New Zealand.

Neptune Hall, in the museum's West Wing, boasts the world's largest ship in a bottle and traces the story of boats from prehistory to modern times. You can also see *Reliant*, a paddle tug built in 1907. After a life cruising up and down the Manchester Ship Canal, she was restored and welded together inside Neptune Hall. Now she's in complete working order, engines and all. *Ooh* and *aah* over Victorian pleasure boats or the triple-expansion steam engine. The Barge House offers time to explore Prince Frederick's gilded and elegant barge, built in 1732 and used by the royal family for more than 100 years. • National Maritime Museum: Romney Rd.; daily except Good Friday, May Day, 24–27 Dec., 1 Jan.; fee (admission includes the Old Royal Observatory and the Meridian, which is at the top of Greenwich Park Hill [Chapter 7, Parks and Gardens]); some disabled access, telephone in advance; 0181-858 4422. ◆

London Transport Museum

The London Transport Museum, tucked into the heart of Covent Garden, is packed with trains, buses, trams, and trolleys, and offers a vast view of London's public transport history. It underwent a $6 million renovation that was completed in 1993. The working exhibits are fascinating. You can try yourself out as a signalperson, flip a switch and watch an early model of an underground lift go into action, and discover what happens when you pull "dead man's handle" on a tube train. • London Transport Museum: Covent Garden tube station; daily except 24–26 Dec.; fee; some handicapped access (and free admission), telephone in advance; 0171-379 6344. ◆

Charles Dickens' House

Dickens' House is a different kind of museum. You'll find lots of the author's memorabilia, portraits, and letters. The rooms look much as they did when Charles Dickens lived there and created characters like Oliver Twist and Ebenezer Scrooge. • Dickens' House Museum: 48 Doughty St.; Russell Square tube station; Mon.–Sat., closed national holidays, 24 Dec.–1 Jan.; fee; 0171-405 2127. ◆

Museum of London

For a look inside Victorian shops or a cell in Newgate Prison, try the Museum of London, just a five-minute walk from either St. Paul's or Barbican tube station. The museum is off street level, so you go up the steps to a high walkway. There's a room for every period of the history of London. The Roman room includes leather shoes, clothes, and artifacts. There's also a model of the Great Fire of London (1666) that lights up for a miniature reenactment of the fire. • Museum of London: Barbican, The City; Tues.–Sat., closed Good Friday, 24–25 Dec.; fee except for late afternoons; wheelchairs available, telephone in advance; 0171-600 3699. ◆

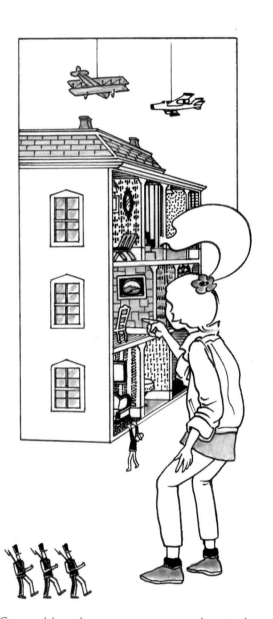

Several London museums are devoted to the treasures of childhood

FOR KIDS OF ALL AGES

Pollock's Toy Museum
is crammed with beautiful toys including dollhouses, tin soldiers, board games, and Victorian toy theaters.
• 1 Scala St: Goodge Street tube station; Mon.-Sat., check for national holiday hours; fee; 0171-636 3452.

London Toy & Model Museum
boasts mechanical toys, tin toys, trains, and other toys that don't start with *T*.
• 23 Craven Hill: Paddington tube station; Tues.–Sat., closed Mondays except national holidays; also closed Good Friday, 24–25 Dec., 1 Jan.; fee; some handicapped access; 0171-262 9450.

Bethnal Green Museum of Childhood has spectacular Russian dolls, rocking horses, and miniature engines on view. Social-history-of-childhood galleries are in progress, and can be seen by appointment. For theater fans, there's an authentic Punch-and-Judy booth.
• Cambridge Heath Road: Bethnal Green tube station; Mon.–Thurs., Sat.; closed May Day, 24–26 Dec., 1 Jan.; 0171-980 4315.

The Roman ruler Caesar called London's great river "Tamesis" and had a wooden bridge built across it. Today the river is called the Thames, and it's a fine place from which to view some of London's best sights,

RIVERS AND BRIDGES

like the Tower Bridge and the Thames Flood Barrier. You can take reasonably priced tour boats up and down the river from Westminster Pier, Charing Cross Pier, the Tower Pier, and Greenwich Pier.

The Tower Bridge Next to the Tower of London, the Tower Bridge opens up its roadway a half-dozen times a week when boats give the signal. Now you can tour inside the bridge. There's the Engine Room Museum, glassed-in overhead walkways, and a massive Victorian steam engine, installed more than 100 years ago to raise and lower the gates, and still pumping. The "Celebration Story" is the new permanent exhibit about the bridge's 100th anniversary, celebrated in 1993. • Tower Bridge Engine Room: an easy walk from Tower Hill Underground; daily except Good Friday, 24–25 Dec., 1 Jan.; fee 0171-403 3761. ◆

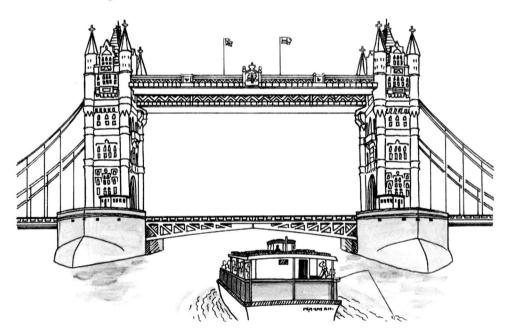

The still-functioning Tower Bridge was built in 1893

*W*hat is London Bridge doing in Lake Havasu, Arizona? The first London Bridge, built by the Romans, was rebuilt many times. Eventually still another, bigger bridge was needed, so the old bridge was sold to Lake Havasu for 1 million pounds.

The Greenwich Waterfront

If you're looking for the "Center of the World," try the borough of **Greenwich,** where you can stand on the zero meridian line (see Chapter 7, Parks and Gardens). There are plenty of fascinating things to see here, along with shopping and eating and just plain meandering on the beautiful streets.

If you get to Greenwich by riverboat, the first thing you can do is climb aboard the dry-docked *Cutty Sark* clipper. Built in 1869, she's a beautiful 280-foot Tea Clipper fully rigged for harbor. On open sea her fastest speed was 17 knots, or about 20 miles per hour. • *Cutty Sark*: Greenwich Pier; daily except 24–26 Dec.; fee; some handicapped access; 0181-858 3445.

Cutty Sark's neighbor is the *Gipsy Moth IV*, famous for a solo round-the-world voyage in 1966–67, when the late Sir Francis Chichester raced her 29,677 miles during 226 days at sea. • *Gipsy Moth IV*: Apr.– Oct.; fee; 0181-858 3445.)

After you've been on the river, try walking under it. The **Greenwich Foot Tunnel** connects Greenwich to Isle of Dogs, which Henry VIII used as a hunting ground and where he kept his royal dogs. On the Greenwich side, you'll enter the drippy tunnel from a small domed building in

Down below deck on the Cutty Sark, you can drop ten pence in the coin slot and hear recorded historical tidbits, or check out the amazing collection of ship's figureheads (the carved and painted wooden figures that decorate a ship's bow)

Cutty Sark Gardens. You'll emerge in Island Gardens, a small park on Isle of Dogs. The isle became the center of the London dockyards in the early 1800s; now it's part of a redevelopment plan. From the park you can easily stroll to Island Garden Station, where the elevated **Docklands Light Railway** stops every ten minutes. Hop aboard with your camera because this train gives you an overhead view of London's

docks, a bit of the ruin and rubble from World War II, and the city of Charles Dickens' famous books. (Small fee.) From Island Gardens it's a good view back to Greenwich. After the ride is over you have to walk all the way back, but it's only a bit longer than the width of the river.

From Greenwich you can catch a boat downriver to the **Thames Flood Barrier,** which has saved London several times. ◆

From afar, the Thames Flood Barrier looks like a series of giant metal monsters, heads raised and eyes blinking green and red. Close up, it takes on an eerie beauty.

River pirates, scuffle hunters, and other thieves cruised the Thames in early days. If you sail along the river past Wapping, look for the Town of Ramsgate, a pub dating from the 1600s. After a nearby trial with a very strict judge, pirates were tied to the pub's pier at low tide. There they stayed for punishment until the waters rose and fell three times. Another historical spot in Wapping is Execution Dock, where Captain Kidd and various other pirates were hanged.

Thames Barrier London is sinking at a rate of 12 inches every century. The lower it gets, the more likely it becomes that the Thames will flood the city. Three hundred people died in 1953 from flooding. The flood barrier, completed in 1983, was constructed so this would never happen again. During construction, 250 divers worked in zero visibility water. The barrier, with ten steel gates, reaches 520 meters from shore to shore. The four main gates each weigh 3,700 tons, and there's a 30-minute maximum closure time. It's best to see the barrier from the river. Then you can go ashore to the Thames Barrier Visitors Centre and see a video, an audiovisual show, and a work-ing model. • Thames Barrier Visitor Centre: fee; handicapped access; 0181-854 1373. If you decide to take the train instead of the boat, the Charlton Train Station is 15 minutes' walk from the Centre. ◆

The Lutine Bell Trading ships traveled on the Thames to and from the open sea. Often, on stormy nights, ships were overdue. The **Lutine Bell** was rung twice if the ship was safe and only once if she was wrecked. The Lloyd's of London building (designed by Richard Rogers), in which the bell is now kept, is no longer open to public view because of threats of terrorism. ◆

The London Tourist Board's **Riverboat Information Services** provides recorded information (including referral numbers) for cruises to and from Westminster Pier, Charing Cross Pier, the Tower Pier, and the Thames Flood Barrier. Call 071-730-4812.

Jugglers, actors, writers, magicians—London has long been a city of entertainment. Theaters abound, some dating back hundreds of years. There's the Haymarket, Prince of Wales, Adelphi, and Her Majesty's, just to name a few. With

THAT'S ENTERTAINMENT

at least 50 major theaters to choose from, you can see shows like *The Phantom of the Opera, Starlight Express, Me and My Girl,* and of course the longest-running show in the world, *The Mousetrap.* London is pure heaven for theater lovers.

Covent Garden   Covent Garden, named for the garden kept by the medieval monks of Westminster Abbey, has a rowdy reputation. In the 1700s the district was known for bawdy houses, pickpockets, and a theater monopoly. Today it's still famous for footlights and greasepaint.

One of Covent Garden's oldest theaters is **Theatre Royal, Drury Lane,** opened in 1663 and frequented by King Charles II. There he watched many an evening's entertainment and fell in love with the actress Nell Gwynne; 071-494 5060.

The **Royal Opera House** on Bow Street is just plain beautiful, with a creamy white and gold auditorium, a proscenium decorated by Raffaelle Monti, and a romantic foyer. If you get a chance, go inside; 071-240 1066.

St. Paul's Church, near the Piazza, is known as the actors' church. The walls are covered with memorials to actors, actresses, and artists. This is where Samuel Pepys watched the first recorded performance of a Punch-and-Judy show in 1662. A plaque marks the spot.

Street entertainment continues today around Covent Garden Central Market, with mimes, magicians, and assorted show-biz folks doing their thing. Inside the market musicians play everything from folk to funky. The tradition of pickpockets continues, so keep an eye on your wallet. • Covent Garden: Covent Garden tube station. ◆

The streets at Covent Garden are often filled with vendors and entertainers

When earls and lords rode to the hounds, the hunting cry was "So-ho!" And that's probably how *Soho*, the area of London directly west of Covent Garden, got its name. In the 17th century, it was a fashionable place to live. Then it became the spot where immigrants decided to settle. When the poor move into areas, the rich often sell their houses and leave. In the 1800s that's what happened, and Soho developed a reputation for music halls, writers, and eccentrics. In the early 20th century, Soho became known as a fashionable "dining area." You can still find great food and nightlife in Soho, but some of the entertainment may not be appropriate for children. • Soho: Piccadilly Circus, Tottenham Court, or Oxford Circus tube stations.

Covent Garden is London's premiere theater district

*Keep your eyes open; you could spot
the next international trend on King's Road*

The **King's Road** in Chelsea used to be exactly that a long time ago—a private road for kings. Then, in the 1960s, it became famous for street entertainment, girls in miniskirts, and long-haired boys in paisley shirts. In the 1970s punk became fashionable, and you can still spot some green and purple mohawks cruising the neighborhoods. But mostly Chelsea is a quiet and pretty residential area nowadays. • Chelsea: Sloane Square or South Kensington tube stations.

*B*ackstage is almost more fun than center stage! Two theaters offer tours behind the scenes: **Royal National Theatre** (South Bank; tours, 0171-633 0880; tickets, 0171-928 2252) and **Barbican Centre**, where the Royal Shakespeare Company is in residence (Silk St.; the Gallery is free and open; guided tours of the Centre and theater are by appointment only, 0171-628 0183 [fee]; handicapped access; Centre, 0171-638 4141).

England's National Theatre

The idea of a national theater was around for a long time in London. But only in 1962 did it become official, with Sir Laurence Olivier, the famous actor, in charge. More than ten years later it moved into its new home across the Thames. The **Royal National Theatre**, at Southbank, includes three theaters: the Olivier, the Lyttleton, and the Cottesloe. It's a fabulous place to see theater, from the classics to the most avant-garde. It's advisable to book seats in advance. • Royal National Theatre: Waterloo tube station; 0171-928 2252. ◆

Little Angel Marionette Theatre offers viewers the chance to watch actors of a smaller persuasion. • 14 Dagmar Passage, Islington; Angel, Highbury, or Islington tube stations; call for opening hours; 0171-226 1787.

Up-to-the-Minute Entertainment Information

Pick up a weekly copy of *Early Times—Independent Newspaper for Young People* as soon as you arrive in London. Written for kids, by kids, it gives you the latest in world news, cartoons, political interviews, and entertainment reviews.

Kidsline, a recorded information service on events that may be of interest to children, is ringable during business hours: 0171-222 8000. ◆

Shopping can be one of the pleasures of traveling. What you find in a city's stores tells you a lot about its people. London

SHOPPING

has some very special stores with novel gifts for friends back home. If you're on a budget, try window-shopping!

Famous Shopping Spots At the world-famous **Harrod's** on Brompton Road, there are odd things to buy, like a toy caterpillar that's 250 feet long and costs almost £6,000. Harrod's is a department store that looks like a palace. Even the Queen of England shops there. Make sure you find the food halls on the ground floor. They sell meat, cheese, and sweets, too. Best of all is the fish hall, where men in aprons carve sculptures out of colorful fresh fish every day. Harrod's toy department is a kid's delight. • Knightsbridge tube station.

Hamley's on Regent Street is a great place for toys, toys, and more toys. Check out the Lego Department to find Buckingham Palace and life-size Beefeaters made out of Lego! You'll also find every kind of action toy imaginable, and some you'd never dream of. • Piccadilly Circus tube station.

A different kind of store in another part of town is **Fortnum & Mason's**, at no. 181 Piccadilly. One of the best things about F&M is keeping track of time. When the famous clock strikes the hour, almost life-size statues of Mr. Fortnum and Mr. Mason glide out of their kiosks and bow to each

If you like to stroll and shop, you'll love Portobello Market

The exchange rate fluctuates in London just like in the rest of the world. When you arrive, you should check at the banks or money exchange for exact rates.

The English monetary system is called the New Pence system.

5 New Pence = 1 Shilling

25 New Pence = 1 Crown

100 New Pence = 1 Pound

other, while 17 bells play old-fashioned tunes. Then Mr. F and Mr. M bow again and disappear back into their kiosks.

You can't go to London without taking real English tea with scones and jam. The restaurant on the ground floor of Fortnum & Mason's is good for that kind of stuff. If you have a real sweet tooth, there's a whole department just for chocolate. • Piccadilly Circus tube station.

Burlington Arcade, near the Royal Academy and Old Bond Street, dates back to 1819, and the storefronts look it. Before you make a spectacle of yourself, read the signs that warn you not to whistle or scream lest the beadles (uniformed attendants) get you! • Piccadilly Circus tube station.

Portobello Market, on Portobello Road, offers strolling shoppers blocks and blocks of things to buy, everything from pricey antiques to flea market items. • Closed on Thursday; Saturday is the big market day. Portobello Road is an easy walk from Nottinghill tube station. ◆

On October 26, 1994, the British pound equaled U.S. $1.6383. Use your calculator to figure this out: U.S. dollars divided by 1.6383 = British pounds; 1.6383 x British pounds = U.S. dollars

London isn't London without sports!
Get ready to enjoy the action.
Remember, in Europe "football" refers

THE SPORTING LIFE

to what Americans know as soccer.
And leave your baseball glove
at home—in England, cricket is king.

Cricket   For a really peculiar and interesting pastime, try **cricket**, the English national game. A cricket game can last five days before a win, lose, or draw. But if you venture out to **Lord's Cricket Ground** on a Sunday afternoon, you're guaranteed about four hours of fun and a probable win or lose. The rules and protocol are puzzling, but you can always find a courteous Londoner in the stands who will explain the basics. You'll find historical highlights and mementos in the Cricket Memorial Gallery on the grounds (open only during the games). For more informal cricket, there are impromptu games during the summer at any recreation ground. • Lord's Cricket Ground: St. John's Wood; Marylebone tube station; 0171-289 1616. ◆

Soccer   Soccer is probably played more often than any other game on the planet. In London (and most of the world) soccer is called football. It's not the same as American football, but it's no different in one respect: people get very emotional about their team. Most stadiums have family cages (screened-in areas) just in case fans get too rowdy. London's teams include the Queen's Park Rangers and the Tottenham Hotspurs, who play at White Hart Lane stadium and are known to their loyal fans as the "Spurs." Division games are played every week from midwinter until May, when the Football Association Cup game is played at Wembley Stadium. Just think of it as London's Superbowl. • Wembley Stadium: Take the train to the Sudbury and Harrow Rd. station in Wembley, Middlesex; for ticket information call 081-900 1234. ◆

Rugby Rugby football (also called rugger) is more like American football than like soccer. There are lots of rugby clubs playing amateur games on weekends. The big professional playoffs include England vs. Scotland and France (in odd-numbered years) and England vs. Wales and Ireland, in the even years. Playoffs take place in January at Twickenham Stadium. • Call 181-892 8161 for general information, 181-744 3111 for tickets. ◆

World-Class Tennis Some of the world's best tennis can be seen every spring at Wimbledon. For tickets, write All England Lawn Tennis and Croquet Club, Church Rd., Wimbledon, London SW19 5AE. Call 081-946 2244 for information. • Take the underground to the Southfields tube station, then board the special bus to Wimbledon. ◆

Horsing Around Epsom Downs offers a chance to enjoy some very English traditions: steeplechase and flat course horse races, and the Derby, the most famous horse race in England. One of the queen's horses often runs but seldom wins. • For information about events at Epsom Downs, call 0372-464 348. Call 071-928 5100 for information on trains to the Downs. ◆

Sportsline is a handy source of information. Call 071-222 8000, weekdays.

Rugby bears some resemblance to American football. Watch for a while, and you'll catch on!

GLOSSARY

How to Speak English   People in London speak English, supposedly . . . but it probably doesn't sound like any English you've heard before. If you try to fit a "bonnet" on your head, you're guaranteed a big headache. And be careful not to drop your "iced lollie" in the "loo" or go outside without your "brolly"!

British	American	British	American
Tube, underground	Subway	Lorry	Truck
Queue	Line (of people)	Tip lorry	Dump truck
Pavement	Sidewalk	Dust bin	Garbage can
Iced lollie	Popsicle	Torch	Flashlight
Knickers	Underpants	Nappies	Diapers
Hooter	Car horn	Lift	Elevator
Biscuits	Cookies	Single ticket	One-way ticket
Sweets	Candy	Ground floor	First floor
Gents or Ladies	Public rest room	Mate	Friend
Loo	Public rest room	Grotty	Dirty
Bathroom	Room for bathing (in a private home)	Cheers	Thanks, good-bye
		Ta	Thanks
Fortnight	Two weeks	Zed	"Z" (the letter)
Brolly	Umbrella	Crisps	Potato chips
Holiday	Vacation	Chips	Fries
Petrol	Gasoline	Tomato catsup	Ketchup
Boot	Trunk (of car)	Quid, Nicker	Pound (English money)
Bonnet	Hood (of car)		
Trousers	Pants	Five "P"	Five pence (English money)
Tart	Pie		
Ironmonger	Hardware store	Flat	Apartment
Chemist	Drugstore	Newsagent	Stand or shop where magazines and news papers are sold
Engaged tone	Busy signal (on telephone)		
Crackers	Fireworks		

CALENDAR OF EVENTS

JANUARY

Rugby: Triple Crown and International Championship at Twickenham Royal Epiphany at Chapel Royal, St James's Palace

Wreath laying at the statue of Charles I, Trafalgar Square, Banqueting Hall

FEBRUARY

Chinese New Year Celebration, Chinatown, Gerard St., Leicester Square

Blessing of Throats, St. Ethelreda, Ely Place

English Folk Dance and Song, Royal Albert Hall

National Canoe Exhibition, Crystal Palace

Pancake Race, Lincoln's Inn Fields

MARCH

Cruft's Dog Show, Birmingham

Oxford and Cambridge Boat Race, Putney to Mortlake

Head of River Races, Putney to Mortlake

Druid Ceremony, Tower Hill

Grimaldi Commemoration Service in honor of the clown, Holy Trinity Church, Dalston

Camden Festival (music and arts), Camden

EASTER

St. Matthew Passion, St. Paul's Cathedral

Butterworth Charity (hot cross buns and money), St. Bartholomew the Great

Presentation by the Queen of Maundy Money (every 4 years), Westminster Abbey

Procession and Carols, Westminster Abbey

Easter Carnival Parade, Battersea Park

London Harness Horse Parade, Regent's Park

APRIL

Westminster Cathedral Spring Flower Festival, Westminster

Beating the Bounds (as in boundary) of the Tower of London

Royal Horticultural Society Spring Flower Show, Royal Horticultural Society Halls, Westminster

London Marathon, Greenwich to Westminster

John Stow Commemoration Service, St. Andrew Undershaft

Signor Pasquale Favale's Marriage Portion, Guildhall

Shakespeare's Birthday Service, Southwark Cathedral

MAY

Royal Windsor Horse Show, Great Park, Windsor

Chelsea Flower Show, Royal Hospital, Chelsea

FA (Football Association) Cup Final, Wembley

London Private Fire Brigades Competition, Guildhall Yard

Lilies and Roses Ceremony, Tower of London

American Memorial Day, Cenotaph, Parliament Square, Westminster Abbey

May Day Rally, Hyde Park

Oak Apple Day Parade, Chelsea Pensioners, Royal Hospital, Chelsea

JUNE

Garter Ceremony, Windsor Castle

Trooping of the Color, Buckingham Palace, Horse Guards

Beating Retreat, Horse Guards Parade, Whitehall

Charles Dickens Commemoration Service, Westminster Abbey

Greenwich Festival (arts, sports, music), Greenwich

All England Lawn Tennis Championships, Wimbledon

The Derby, Epsom Downs
Cricket Test Match, Lord's Cricket Ground
Royal Ascot, Berkshire

JULY
Royal International Horse Show, Wembley
Henry Wood Promenade Concerts, Royal Albert Hall
Benson and Hedges Cup Final, Lord's Cricket Ground
Doggett's Coat and Badge Race, London Bridge to
    Chelsea Bridge
The City Festival, City churches and halls
Swan-Upping, Temple Stairs at Tower Bridge,
    Henley
Lambeth Country Show, Brockwell Park
Mall March, Mall Horse Guards
Metropolitan Police Horse Show and Tournament,
    Imber Court, East Molesey

AUGUST
Hampstead Heath Fair, Hampstead Heath
Greater London Horse Show, Clapham Common
Presentation of a Boar's Head, Smithfield
Children's Books of the Year Show, National Book
    League
European Festival of Model Railways, Central Hall,
    Westminster
Test Match, Oval Cricket Ground
Notting Hill Festival, around Portobello Road

SEPTEMBER
Election of the Lord Mayor, Guildhall, Mansion
    House
Battle of Britain Day, Greater London, Westminster
    Abbey
British Gymnastics Championships, Wembley

OCTOBER
Horse of the Year Show, Wembley
National Brass Band's Championship, Royal Albert
    Hall
Opening of Michaelmas Law Term: Procession of
    Judges, Westminster Abbey
Quits Rents Ceremony, Law Courts
Harvest-of-the-Sea Thanksgiving, St. Mary-at-Hill
Trafalgar Day Ceremony, Trafalgar Square

Notting Hill Festival

NOVEMBER
Remembrance Sunday, Cenotaph, Whitehall
Lord Mayor's Procession and Show, Guildhall,
    Strand, Law Courts
London Film Festival
State Opening of Parliament, Buckingham Palace,
    House of Lords, Westminster
Guy Fawkes Night (with fireworks), Battersea Park,
    Crystal Palace Park, Burgess Park
Veteran Car Run, Hyde Park Corner to Brighton

DECEMBER
Lighting of the Norwegian Christmas Tree, Trafalgar
    Square
Tower of London Parade, Tower of London
Midnight Eucharist, Southwark Cathedral
Watch-night Service, St. Paul's Cathedral
Watch-night Service, Westminster Abbey
Winter Ice Show, Wembley Arena
New Year's Eve Celebrations, Trafalgar Square

INDEX

from John Muir Publications

Kidding Around Series
Family Travel Guides

All of the titles listed below are 64 pages and $9.95 except for *Kidding Around the National Parks* and *Kidding Around Spain*, which are 108 pages and $12.95.

Kidding Around Atlanta, 2nd ed.
Kidding Around Boston, 2nd ed.
Kidding Around Chicago, 2nd ed.
Kidding Around the Hawaiian Islands
Kidding Around London, 2nd ed.
Kidding Around Los Angeles
Kidding Around the National Parks
  of the Southwest
Kidding Around New York City, 2nd ed.
Kidding Around Paris, 2nd ed.
Kidding Around Philadelphia
Kidding Around San Diego
Kidding Around San Francisco
Kidding Around Santa Fe
Kidding Around Seattle
Kidding Around Spain
Kidding Around Washington, D.C., 2nd ed.

X-ray Vision Series

Each title in the series is 8½" x 11", 48 pages, $9.95 paperback, with four-color photographs and illustrations and written by Ron Schultz.

Looking Inside the Brain
Looking Inside Cartoon Animation
Looking Inside Caves and Caverns
Looking Inside Sports Aerodynamics
Looking Inside Sunken Treasure
Looking Inside Telescopes and the
  Night Sky

Masters of Motion Series

Each title in the series is 10¼" x 9", 48 pages, $9.95 paperback, with four-color photographs and illustrations.

How to Drive an Indy Race Car
How to Fly a 747
How to Fly the Space Shuttle

Rainbow Warrior Artists Series

Each title is written by Reavis Moore with a foreword by LeVar Burton, and is 8½" x 11", 48 pages, $14.95 hardcover and $9.95 paperback, with color photographs and illustrations.

Native Artists of Africa
Native Artists of Europe
Native Artists of North America

Crafty Creatures Series

NEW SERIES

Each title in the series is 8½" x 11", 32 pages, and $9.95 hardcover and $5.95 paperback, with full-color photographs and illustrations.

Available September 1995:
Crafty Creatures in Your House
Crafty Creatures in Your Neighborhood
Crafty Creatures in the Wetlands

Extremely Weird Series

All of the titles are written by Sarah Lovett, 8½" x 11", 48 pages, $9.95 paperback and $14.95 hardcover.

Extremely Weird Bats
Extremely Weird Birds
Extremely Weird Endangered Species
Extremely Weird Fishes
Extremely Weird Frogs
Extremely Weird Insects
Extremely Weird Mammals
Extremely Weird Micro Monsters
Extremely Weird Primates
Extremely Weird Reptiles
Extremely Weird Sea Creatures
Extremely Weird Snakes
Extremely Weird Spiders

Kids Explore Series

Each title is written by kids, for kids, by the Westridge Young Writers Workshop, 7" x 9", with photographs and illustrations by the kids.

Kids Explore America's African
  American Heritage
  128 pages, $9.95 paperback
Kids Explore America's Hispanic
  Heritage
  112 pages, $9.95 paperback
Kids Explore America's Japanese
  American Heritage
  144 pages, $9.95 paperback
Kids Explore the Gifts of Children With
  Special Needs
  128 pages, $9.95 paperback
Kids Explore the Heritage of Western
  Native Americans
  128 pages, $9.95 paperback

Bizarre & Beautiful Series

Each title is 8½" x 11", 48 pages, $9[95] paperback and $14.95 hardcover, w[ith] four-color photographs and illustratio[ns]

Bizarre & Beautiful Ears
Bizarre & Beautiful Eyes
Bizarre & Beautiful Feelers
Bizarre & Beautiful Noses
Bizarre & Beautiful Tongues

Rough and Ready Series

Each title is 48 pages, 8½" x 11", $12[.95] hardcover and $9.95 paperback, wi[th] two-color illustrations and duotone archival photographs.

Rough and Ready Cowboys
Rough and Ready Homesteaders
Rough and Ready Loggers
Rough and Ready Outlaws and Law[men]
Rough and Ready Prospectors
Rough and Ready Railroaders

American Origins Series

Each title is 48 pages, 8½" x 11", $12.95 hardcover, with two-color illu[stra]tions and duotone archival photogra[phs]

Tracing Our English Roots
Tracing Our German Roots
Tracing Our Irish Roots
Tracing Our Italian Roots
Tracing Our Japanese Roots
Tracing Our Jewish Roots
Tracing Our Polish Roots

Environmental Titles

Habitats: Where the Wild Things Liv[e]
8½" x 11", 48 pages, color illustratio[ns]
$9.95 paper

The Indian Way: Learning to
  Communicate with Mother Earth
7" x 9", 114 pages, two-color illustra[]tions, $9.95 paper

Rads, Ergs, and Cheeseburgers: The [ ]
  Guide to Energy and the Environm[ent]
7" x 9", 108 pages, two-color illustra[]tions, $13.95 paper

The Kids' Environment Book: What's [ ]
  Awry and Why
7" x 9", 192 pages, two-color illustra[]tions, $13.95 paper